GLADIATOR

MARC TYLER NOBLEMAN

Chicago, Illinois

© 2008 Raintree
Published by Raintree,
A division of Reed Elsevier Inc.
Chicago, Illinois

Customer Service 888-454-2279

Visit our website at www.heinemannraintree.com

Designed by Victoria Bevan, Steve Mead,
 and Bigtop
Printed and bound in China by Leo Paper Group

12 11 10 09 08
10 9 8 7 6 5 4 3 2 1

**Library of Congress
Cataloging-in-Publication Data**
Nobleman, Marc Tyler.
   Gladiator / Marc Tyler Nobleman.
      p. cm. -- (Atomic)
   Includes bibliographical references and index.
   ISBN 978-1-4109-2976-1 (lib. bdg. - hardcover)
-- ISBN 978-1-4109-2997-6 (pbk.)
   1. Gladiators--Juvenile literature. I. Title.
   GV35.N63 2007
   796'.0937--dc22

                                2006101213

Acknowledgments

The author and publisher are grateful to the
following for permission to reproduce copyright
material: akg-images pp. **22** (Peter Connolly), **14**
bottom, **21**; Alamy Images/Arco Images (The Kobal
Collection) p. **13**; Bridgeman Art Library p. **6**; Corbis
pp. **26–27** (Sygma/Alberto Pizzoli), **29** (TempSport/
Dimitri Lundt); Dreamworks/Universal/The Kobal
Collection/Jaap Buitendijk p. **14** top; Masterfile/
David Schmidt p. **18**; Rex Features/Sipa Press p. **17**;
The Art Archive pp. **5** (Museo della Civilta Romana
Rome/Dagli Orti), **20** (Galleria Borghese Rome/Dagli
Orti), **25** (Museo di Capodimonte, Naples/Dagli
Orti); The Kobal Collection/Universal/Bryna p. **9**.

Cover photograph of gladiators in the arena at the
Europa leisure park, Rust, Germany, reproduced with
permission of Rex Features (Richard Gardner).

Photo research by Mica Brancic
Illustrations by Jeff Edwards and Paul McCaffrey

The publishers would like to thank Nancy Harris,
Dee Reid, and Diana Bentley for their assistance in
the preparation of this book.

Every effort has been made to contact copyright
holders of any material reproduced in this book.
Any omissions will be rectified in subsequent
printings if notice is given to the publishers.

Contents

Some words are printed in bold, **like this**. You can find out what they mean in the glossary. You can also look in the box at the bottom of the page where the word first appears.

WHAT IS A GLADIATOR?

Swords were always swinging in ancient Rome. While soldiers waged wars in distant parts of the large Roman Empire, gladiators fought each other in the cities.

A gladiator was a professional fighter in ancient Rome. Gladiators fought one another in massive **amphitheaters** in front of thousands of spectators. The crowds cheered them on, much like people do at modern sporting events. They were cheering for an entertaining match—and sometimes for blood.

How did gladiator games begin?

The first known gladiator contest was held at a cattle market in 264 B.C.E., when three pairs of slaves owned by wealthy citizens battled each other. The purpose of the fight was to honor another wealthy man who had died. Over the years, gladiator contests changed from private funeral rituals to public crowd-pleasers.

amphitheater	large, circular stadium in which entertainment events are held
empire	group of countries under one ruler

Gladiator Fact!

Gladiator games were popular for 700 years. The Colosseum in Rome (below) was the most important amphitheater for gladiator battles.

Europe

W. Asia

Rome

Mediterranean Sea

N. Africa

| 0 | 1,000 miles |
| 0 | 1,000 km |

The purple areas on this map show the extent of the Roman Empire in around 300 C.E.

The people of ancient Rome considered fighting and bravery to be very important.

WHO BECAME GLADIATORS?

Most gladiators were slaves, criminals, or prisoners of war. Their owners or captors forced them to fight as gladiators.

Gladiators had a double life in ancient Rome. Since many came from low levels of society, some people regarded them as slaves. Yet others considered them heroes. Gladiators were similar to warriors, top athletes, and movie stars all at the same time.

Could a person choose to be a gladiator?

Free men could also become gladiators. They were paid just to sign up and were often paid again if they won. Many volunteered because they were poor, while others wanted the glory that a successful gladiator received.

captor   person who captures another

GLADIATOR SCHOOL

Slaves, criminals, and prisoners of war were taught to be gladiators at schools called *ludi*. A *lanista* trained them, sometimes for one year. They used wooden swords and practiced with dummies stuffed with straw.

What was life like in gladiator school?

Gladiators in training had to work hard, but in some ways they were treated well. They ate three daily meals, exercised regularly, and were cared for by excellent doctors. Gladiators were expensive; *lanistas* wanted to keep them healthy so they could fight well.

At one school, a slave named Spartacus started a rebellion of gladiators and slaves. They battled Roman armies for two years, and beat some of them—but were eventually defeated.

lanista	person who trained gladiators in ancient Rome

Gladiator Fact!

The largest gladiator school in Rome was connected to the Colosseum (see pages 14 and 15) by an underground tunnel.

Most contests were between two gladiators, but sometimes bigger groups fought each other.

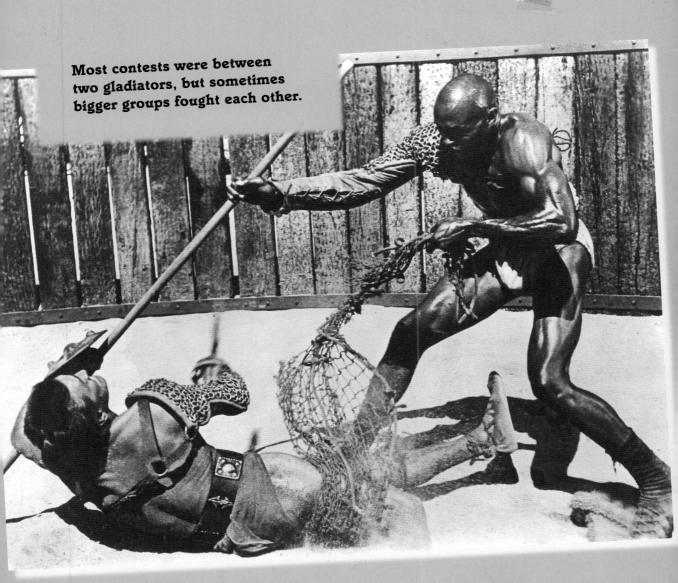

Murmillo

Retiarius

Samnite/Secutor

Thracian

Samnites and Thracians were named after groups of people whom Rome had conquered.

Types of Gladiator

Many gladiators were large—maybe even overweight—men. Like modern wrestlers, gladiators all dressed differently in order to create a strange cast of "characters" in the arena.

Four types of gladiators were the most common:

1 The *Samnite* wore more armor than any other gladiator. He carried a large, rectangular shield like a Roman soldier, and a short metal sword.

2 The *Thracian* carried a curved dagger and a small, round shield.

3 The *Retiarius* had little armor and no sword or shield. He carried a net to **snare opponents**, as well as a **trident**. Unlike other gladiators, he had no helmet.

4 The *Murmillo* had a helmet shaped like a fish and carried a straight sword and a large shield.

opponent — person one fights
snare — to catch in a net
trident — spear with three sharp points

Were there other popular gladiators?

Other types of gladiator were stranger still. Some were named after the weapons or **strategies** they used. Their names come from the now-**dead language** of Latin.

The *Laquearius* tried to rope his **opponent** with a lasso, but possibly carried no other weapons. The *Velite* had a spear attached to a strap, so he could pull it back after he threw it.

The *Secutor* resembled the *Samnite*. He wore an egg-shaped helmet that had two eyeholes, and he was known for chasing opponents around the arena.

The *Andabata* wore a helmet without eyeholes. In other words, he fought blind!

Gladiator Fact!

Graffiti on ancient walls reveals that women had crushes on gladiators. One gladiator was described as making "all the girls sigh."

Gladiators did not always fight on foot. The *Essedarii* fought from a **chariot**. The *Eques* fought on horseback, using a **lance**, as in this modern reconstruction.

chariot	carriage with wheels that is pulled by horses
dead language	language that is no longer commonly spoken
lance	long, pointed weapon
strategy	the way a person plans to do something

Sometimes in the Colosseum hunted animals ended up killing their hunters.

Romans sometimes filled the center of the Colosseum with water to watch criminals fight in ships!

A Day at the Amphitheater

The most famous amphitheater where gladiators fought was the Colosseum in Rome, which was then called the Flavian Amphitheater. Romans celebrated its opening in 80 B.C.E with 100 days of games.

The Colosseum held 50,000 spectators. The arena floor was covered in sand—to absorb spilled blood.

What was the fight schedule?

On a typical day, the amphitheater had three shows. In the morning, men and women hunted exotic wild animals such as lions, alligators, elephants, and even ostriches. Technically, these people were not gladiators. At noon, criminals were killed, often in horrific ways such as being burned alive. The afternoon offered the main event: gladiator fights.

THE PRESHOW

Gladiators entered the arena in a parade, sometimes led by the most popular gladiator on a chariot. Jugglers and acrobats came with them.

The gladiators stopped before the **editor**, the person who organized the contests. The editor was often the **emperor** himself.

Did the fighting start right away?

To warm up the crowd, gladiators performed fake fights, probably using wooden swords. Then, inspectors made sure that their metal swords were sharp.

When a trumpet sounded, it was time for real battle. Gladiators drew lots to determine the order in which they would fight.

Most contests were between two gladiators, but bigger groups also sometimes battled.

editor   person who organized gladiator games in ancient Rome

emperor   ruler of ancient Rome

Gladiators paraded in front of the emperor and audience before each contest.

Gladiator Fact!

Movies show gladiators shouting to the emperor, "We who are about to die salute you." However, it is not likely that gladiators said this regularly.

Musicians played flutes and drums during the fights. When the combat sped up, so did the music.

Gladiator Fact!

After analyzing gladiator bones, scientists believe gladiators probably fought barefoot.

THE FIGHT

Gladiators usually did not fight their own kind. For example, a *Retiarius* and *Secutor* would face each other. The *Retiarius* wore less protection than the *Secutor*, but the *Secutor's* heavier armor slowed him down.

Did gladiator fights have limits?

Though fighting pairs had different weapons and **combat** styles, they were evenly matched. The crowd did not want to see a strong gladiator fight a weak one; an unfair battle is boring.

Gladiator combat had no rounds or time restrictions. However, some historians think the fights had rules, such as no sneak attacks.

Gladiator trainers yelled advice. If a gladiator showed fear, his trainer might whip him.

combat fight or battle

Gladiators did not have to die in every battle.
Fights ended in one of three ways:

1. A gladiator was killed.

2. The audience called for the battle to stop, in order to reward gladiators who fought well.

3. A gladiator asked for mercy by dropping his weapons and raising his left index finger.

What happened if a gladiator asked for his life to be spared?

Audience members used hand gestures to show whether they wanted a gladiator to live or die. The **editor** made the final decision. The editor usually did what the audience requested.

Left-handed gladiators (like the one on the left) had an advantage. Right-handed gladiators were less prepared for an attack from that side.

The crowd turned their thumbs one way to mean "release him," and another way to mean "kill him." Today, no one is quite sure which way delivered the gladiators' death sentence.

Gladiator Fact!

Each gladiator typically fought only two or three times a year.

Some Romans believed that watching gladiator fights brought out a brutal side in people.

THE AUDIENCE

Spectators at gladiator fights did more than observe. They also had a role in the show. In ancient Rome, some people were not allowed to vote in political elections. At the gladiator fights, however, everyone could vote.

How else did the crowd take part?

When a gladiator was injured, the crowd screamed, *"Habet, hoc habet!"* (Latin for "He's had it!"). Sometimes they screamed, *"Mitte!"* ("Let him go!"). If they were not pleased, they might scream, *"Lugula!"* ("Kill him!").

In the **amphitheater**, people sat according to their position in society. Rich men were closer to the action in the arena, while poorer people were behind them. Women sat in the back. Spectators could bring a picnic lunch or buy food such as stuffed pastries at the amphitheater.

After the Fight

The audience expected a gladiator to die without displaying fear. He would kneel and hold the thigh of the winner, who would stab him in the neck with his sword.

Two men came out to confirm for the audience that the loser was not faking his death. One poked him with a hot iron rod and the other struck him with a hammer. A slave then dragged the body out.

What was the prize?

The victor was awarded a palm branch and sometimes coins donated by the audience. Gladiators who performed especially well received a **laurel** crown. However, the best award was freedom. If a gladiator survived long enough, he might be a free man.

laurel   glossy, evergreen plant

Arenas had separate exits for winners, for defeated gladiators who were spared, and for the dead.

Tombstones still standing in Rome show how many victories certain gladiators had—in some cases, as many as 150.

GLADIATORS NO MORE

Most men were killed in their first year as a gladiator. Some lasted longer, but still died young.

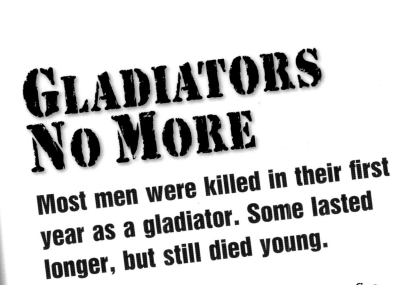

A gladiator who managed to survive for up to five years might be permitted to retire. At that time, an **editor** might honor him by presenting him with a wooden sword called a *rudis*.

What did a retired gladiator do?

Some retired gladiators were employed as bodyguards for politicians or wealthy people. Others worked at schools that trained new gladiators.

Banned

In 404 C.E. spectators stoned a monk to death as he tried to stop a gladiator fight. As a result, **Emperor** Honorius banned gladiator games. An **era** of senseless bloodshed was finally over.

era   **period of time**

MODERN GLADIATORS

In the modern world, humans no longer battle to the death to amuse others. However, some modern contact sports can lead to serious injuries—and occasionally death.

Which modern sports involve violence?

In boxing, two people wearing cushioned gloves repeatedly punch each other, in an attempt to knock each other down. The gloves may be soft, but the pummeling is hard.

In wrestling, one person attempts to pin another to a mat so he or she cannot move. In football, teams play defense by tackling the person with the ball.

Yet when crowds cheer in stadiums today, they want goals, not gore.

Modern wrestlers compete
with muscles, not weapons.

Gladiator Fact!

One controversial modern sport
does end with a killing—but
not of a person. In bullfighting,
people called *toreros* perform
with, and eventually kill, a bull
in front of an audience.

Glossary

amphitheater large, circular stadium in which entertainment events are held

captor person who captures another

chariot carriage with wheels that is pulled by horses

combat fight or battle

dead language language that is no longer commonly spoken

editor person who organized gladiator games in ancient Rome

emperor ruler of ancient Rome

empire group of countries under one ruler

era period of time

lance long, pointed weapon

lanista person who trained gladiators in ancient Rome

laurel glossy, evergreen plant

opponent person one fights

snare to catch in a net

strategy the way a person plans to do something

trident spear with three sharp points

Want to Know More?

Books

✳ Frew, Katherine. *Gladiators: Battling in the Arena.* New York: Children's Press, 2005.

✳ Malam, John. *You Wouldn't Want to Be a Roman Gladiator!* New York: Franklin Watts, 2000.

Websites

✳ www.pbs.org/wnet/warriorchallenge/gladiators/profile.html
Read profiles of the different kinds of gladiator.

✳ www.pbs.org/wnet/warriorchallenge/gladiators/interactive_flash.html
An interactive tour of the Colosseum.

✳ www.salariya.com/web_books/gladiator/index.html
Learn some gory facts about what it was like to be a gladiator.

If you liked this Atomic book, why don't you try these...?

Index